C000149109

Uncovered

Mission: To Proclaim Transformation and Truth

Publisher: Transformed Publishing, Cocoa, FL

Website: www.transformedpublishing.com

Email: transformedpublishing@gmail.com

Copyright © 2023 by Babette Bailey

All rights reserved solely by the author. No part of this book may be reproduced, stored in a retrieval system, or transmitted in any form or by any means without expressed written permission of the author.

This work is based on the author's life experiences and personal study. It aligns with Biblical teaching, not medical or mental health expertise.

Scriptures are taken from the New King James Version ®. Copyright © 1982 by Thomas Nelson. Used by permission. All rights reserved.

ISBN: 978-1-953241-42-9

Uncovered

Babette Bailey

Table of Contents

Introduction

The thoughts and what I want to portray most about *Uncovered,* are how easy it is to take for granted having a covering, and the devastation we often overlook that can result when we're uncovered. And no matter what season we're in, where we are in the world, or who we are; we all need to be covered. I think it's one of those things we don't think enough about until we realize we are without a covering. I don't think we realize how much we need to be covered until we start to mature and understand our nakedness, our vulnerability, our aloneness, and all the affects that can arise from being uncovered, as well as other major and lasting impacts it can have on our lives.

I happened to overhear one of my friends and her husband having a conversation one day. I don't remember all the details, but I do remember he was saying something to her about staying safe, and she seemed a little annoyed by it. Whatever it was, I know he was looking out for her best interest, and it made me think of how I would love to have someone looking out for me that way. What I saw was how her husband was covering her. I think what she saw was too much cover, or him being overbearing. I have seen them interact many times before. I've always known him to be the kind of man and husband who would go to bat for her. He would never tolerate any form of disrespect to her from anyone! But this day, it was as if it was magnified to me. It made me sense how much I felt the pain and the struggle of being without that type of covering. I think she became a lot more aware of how special it was to have that kind of attention when I told her how much I longed for that kind of covering.

I think people often feel like they would love to have that until they get it; and I understand how easy it can be to have it and take it for granted. Too many times, as they say, "We don't miss the water till the well runs dry."

Anyway, knowing her, I know her reaction was not any form of rejection to her husband, nor any form of disrespect. I just think sometimes we can miss *it* being in our own feelings. Sometimes we don't want the cover pulled up, we just want it down by our feet or next to us. It can make us too hot or uncomfortable. Even while that may be true, I don't think that's the real issue. It's usually not what we say, it's how we say it. I've learned we must always strive to be careful at how we say, "No-thank you."

There was another incident that happened between my Bishop and his sister that I think is an awesome display of a beautiful covering of love. He has often shared the story of how one of his sisters got tangled up with a "knuckle dragger," that's what he calls the guy. He basically stepped in to keep her from getting tangled up, in what he perceived to be a bad situation. He could see beyond all the fluff and the psychological manipulation so many women fall for; and he challenged the guy's motives toward real love. When it came down to it, the guy ended up moving on because he realized she was not alone. She was covered. He wasn't going to just be able to get in her head and run game like he could on someone who was alone. I love hearing that story.

It is always amazing to see fathers, brothers, uncles, cousins, even other men watch out for ladies that way; especially the younger ladies who are so vulnerable, inexperienced, gullible, innocent, un-assuming, who desire and can truly appreciate someone trying to protect them.

That makes me think about Jacob's sons Simeon and Levi, who were outraged when their sister Dinah was raped. Even though the young man wanted to marry her and make things right, it wasn't enough for them. In their eyes, he had dishonored Dinah and mishandled her. I think many people may struggle with how the brothers reacted, but what I admire is how much they cared. They were enraged at the

3

thought of him uncovering her, bringing shame and disgrace to her, and ultimately pain and anxiety. *The brothers' covering!* I know there are still many brothers who will go the distance to protect their sisters, also many fathers and other men. I don't think however, there are nearly enough fathers, mothers, brothers, uncles, teachers, leaders, caregivers, mentors, friends, etc., who really care enough to do something about it. How many children could be spared from predators and even from the consequences of their own foolish decisions if they had that level of guidance and protection? How many ladies could have the hope of being in fulfilling, happy and proper marriages, instead of being unwed mothers, single parents, caught up with married men, treated like harlots, and even worse, whores?

I'm sure even as I begin to delve into this sensitive and serious topic, your wheels are already spinning. Many of us have felt the shame and the pain of being uncovered. But it is my hope that in sharing my thoughts and my heart about being uncovered, it will not only provoke us all to do a better job of covering others, but also make us more mindful of how important it is to be covered, protected, and safe; realizing how vulnerable we become when we are not.

While there are times we are violated because we are uncovered, there are also times when we refuse to be covered. We can refuse God's help and step out of His will. We can go against the purposes of God and His righteousness. We can rebel against the coverings God provides through parents, grand-parents, leaders, other family members, friends, or even the wisdom to cover ourselves. Often, it's not until we look back and realize what we couldn't see before or see one of our loved ones making the same bad decisions we've made, that we conclude, it wasn't others who failed to cover us, but we refused to be covered.

We've all had times we didn't appreciate being covered: being told what to do and not to do; how to dress and how not to dress; where to go and what we should avoid; etc.

When we are uncovered, however we end up uncovered, we feel the shame, the pain, the conse-quences, etc. of being out of that safe place.

Chapter One
A Spiritual Covering

I want to start off chapter one discussing our spiritual covering. This may seem to some to be the obvious, and like it goes without saying that *we need a spiritual covering.* But, taking a step back to really look at things from a spiritual aspect, I realize we are more exposed than we really give enough attention to. The Bible tells us in Luke 22:3 that Satan entered Judas. Was it because he was not truly under the covering as the other disciples were? Was it because of the rebellious condition of his heart or the sinful things he desired that caused him to remove himself from the covering of God? In Luke 22:32, Jesus prayed for Peter, that his faith would not fail. Peter knew he needed to be covered. I believe Peter's heart and his motives made the difference in Jesus' prayers and actions toward him versus Judas. Jesus prayed for all the disciples, and for all people. Romans 8:34 reminds us, ". . . It is Christ who died, and furthermore is also risen, who is even at the right hand of God, who also makes intercession for us." Be assured, there is always someone praying for *us.* We are all vulnerable and susceptible to the principalities, wickedness, and evil forces of darkness. In 1 Corinthians 10:12, we are admonished to be careful when we think we stand, lest we fall.

That's why we all need to be covered in prayer, and we all need to be careful to do our best to remain under that covering.

I was in a situation where I was continuously reminded to be careful, just like that Scripture speaks about. Like my friend, I was somewhat annoyed by what I felt to be an overbearing and unnecessary attempt to cover me. I was convinced I was stronger than I was. As things transpired, I did fall, utterly! I couldn't believe it! There were even times when I could feel I was falling, but by the time I tried to compose myself, the momentum was already too strong and moving too fast to just hit the brakes. James 1:15 warns us, "Then, when desire has conceived, it gives birth to sin; and sin, when it is full-grown, brings forth death." More simply, "Sin, when it is full blown brings forth death." I know that's what happens when there is infidelity, fornication, pornography, and any form of temptation. Many think they can just stay on the surface and not get completely immersed, but all it takes is a little taste, or one time, or even one thought. That's why this Scripture speaks so loudly to me when I read it, and why it continues to reverberate in my spirit every time I read it or hear it. I have learned temptation is nothing to be played with or taken lightly. I believe it takes more than just having a fear of man. As the old folks used to say, "We need to have the fear of God put in us." No, we don't want to feel like God is waiting to strike us down every time we make a wrong decision, but we don't need to feel like we can just do whatever we want without understanding how great the consequences can be neither. We must understand there are natural repercussions as well as spiritual. Especially when there are others involved or others who can be greatly affected and impacted by our choices and mistakes.

We all love the story of Esther, and there's so much to be said about this amazing woman. But what I love so much about this story is how Mordecai, her uncle, took her in and covered her. She lost her mother and father, but she was not uncovered. Mordecai raised her as if she was his own daughter. But not only did he cover her, she gratefully accepted and stayed under his protection, submitting to his teaching and his guidance. She obeyed him. She respected him. She did not despise his correction and discipline. This story speaks to how even though our natural parents may not be able to cover us or care for us as they should, God will step in or send someone who will. His compassion never fails.

A father of the fatherless, a defender of widows, *is* God in His holy habitation. God sets the solitary in families . . .
-Psalm 68:5-6

We need to have the humility, the respect, and the appreciation to receive and reap the benefits made available to us.

There are many people doing their best to cover others; parents, mentors, leaders, teachers, etc., whom they see as exposed or ignorant to the potential trouble and dangers that surround them. Pastors and preachers are there doing all they can to open the spiritual eyes of our understanding and guide everyone by the Spirit of God, and so people will not be consumed by sinful and fleshly desires, nor the evils of this world. And hats off to those leaders who will indeed protect the flock from wolves, especially those who will challenge those who would prey on the weak and unsuspecting. Unfortunately, some are weak and vulnerable, and some are easily manipulated and need those who would dare to intervene on their behalf.

For those of us who are in Christ Jesus, it is heart wrenching to see our children move from the umbrella of the protection we try to provide; the protection that God provides through His promises and the wisdom and insights of His Word; and even just the protection afforded from endeavoring to keep the natural and worldly laws of man. Often, we can see the enemy moving among *other* people: children, family, friends, etc., and it may be hard to get them to see or understand spiritual things, especially when they are so tangled up in the emotions of their situations. I imagine that our parents and others have felt the same about us, when we were the ones tangled up. But like I already mentioned; we are all susceptible. There are times when we all fail to see clearly, hear clearly, or when we are not listening to the voice of God or anybody else who may be challenging our desires and our decisions. We're often just too consumed by the deception, the lures, and the lies of the enemy. In those times, we don't want to hear, and we choose not to listen.

Unfortunately, like Queen Vashti who was dethrone-ed from being the queen and whose actions caused her to lose everything, sometimes the consequences of our choices and actions can affect the rest of our lives. Our wrong decisions can happen one too many times (*see* Esther 1).

I pray we would all strive to see our covering as the full armor of God mentioned in Ephesians 6:13-18:

> Therefore take up the whole armor of God, that you may be able to withstand in the evil day, and having done all, to stand. Stand therefore, having girded your waist with truth, having put on the breastplate of righteousness, and having shod your feet

with the preparation of the gospel of peace; above all, taking the shield of faith with which you will be able to quench all the fiery darts of the wicked one. And take the helmet of salvation, and the sword of the Spirit, which is the word of God; praying always with all prayer and supplication in the Spirit, being watchful to this end with all perseverance and supplication for all the saints—

Our belt of truth protects our loins and reproduction organs from multiplying ungodly desires. Our breastplate of righteousness protects our vital organs - hearts, lungs, veins, arteries, etc. that if damaged, without a miracle, our lives would be lost. Jesus' righteousness freed us from the bondage of sin which produces death. Our feet prepared with the readiness of the Gospel of peace keeps us vigilant as we choose what steps to take. Our shield of faith is necessary to block every fiery dart of the enemy trying to stop us from moving forward. Our helmet of salvation guards our minds (thoughts, desires, imaginations, memories, and more). Our Sword of the Spirit is the Word of God. The full armor of God is a very intricate part of God's spiritual covering. It is readily available to all who will receive it.

I would like to take this opportunity to thank God for His extremely amazing and loving covering He provides for us all; after we've lost our innocence; after the shame and the disgrace; after the violations; after the rebellion and the wayward decisions. Thank God for the warmth of His compassion: for healing our wounds, covering our nakedness, the protection He provides even when we fail to see it or fail to acknowledge it, when we cast it off as too over-bearing or unwanted. I pray for all to reconsider our attitude, our outlook, and our response to God's amazing covering readily available to us, through us, and for us.

I believe we are all vulnerable to potential spiritual attacks and we all need the covering of a spiritual father or mother watching over our soul, and even the connectedness, prayer, and covering of brothers and sisters in the church family. Before I ever had that kind of covering, I didn't think about it. But since I've had *it*, there is a void I feel when I don't have it.

I imagine this is how kids feel when they become adults and have to leave home. They part from mom and dad and must learn to navigate for themselves, even cover themselves naturally and spiritually, also when there is a need for growth or separation, causing us to make necessary adjustments. Sometimes I don't think we realize how much we may depend on spiritual leaders until they are not there. While we may depend on our pastors and leaders, even each other to a certain extent, spiritually I know God must be the One in whom our dependency truly lies.

With all that said, I would also like to say, be careful if you are the one who others are relying on, or if you are the one leading others on God's behalf. You can truly make a difference, negatively or positively, by what you do and don't do. *Lord, help us all!* It is truly a great responsibility to be a spiritual leader, covering, or influence.

Chapter Two
A Parental Covering

As a parent, I have literally fought with my children trying to keep them from doing things I knew would cause them to be dangerously, vulnerably, and improperly exposed. When they were younger it seemed easier. I could dress them and decide what they would and would not wear. I could decide, for the most part, where they could and could not go; what they could and could not do. But the older they got, the harder it became to keep them under my rule and my influence.

I tried explaining why my feelings were the way they were. I tried telling them of the dangers and potential problems that could come from the things they were wanting to do and the choices they were making. I tried reasoning with them, and even allowing others to share their perspectives with them, hoping that if they thought I was just being overprotective and unreasonable, maybe they would listen to others who they loved and respected, and who they knew loved them. I tried giving them a little more room to grow. I pointed out others whose lives had been devastated by doing some of the same things they were doing and going down some of the same paths they were choosing. Sometimes, I believe I was successful. Other times, I don't know if I didn't pray hard enough, didn't fight for them hard enough, or didn't try long enough. It felt like all I could do was take a step back, like the father with his prodigal son (*see* Luke 15:11-32), hoping one day they would come to themselves and return home.

I know I'm not alone. I've heard many stories and seen many parents cry over their children. I don't know if we will ever get beyond the emotions we feel behind their failures and their painful mistakes. I believe no matter what they do and how bad their issues can be, they are always an extension of us. Because of that, even when we are angry with them, or they completely turn their backs on us, we still love them and cry over them. We still hurt when they hurt and cry when they cry, and we still rejoice when they succeed.

Absalom, one of David's sons was determined to take the kingdom from his own father, King David. He was so rebellious and disrespectful, even still David wept bitterly when Absalom was killed in the battle he was fighting, trying to destroy David. Who can understand *this* love? I think deep down we all can. Many of us have put our children out of the house; we have determined to cut them off; and we have been so hurt and angered by them that we didn't want to love them. *Still,* if their lives were to

16

come to an end, we would feel much of the same pain David felt when Absalom's life ended.

I believe this is the kind of love God has for His children. I believe like Absalom, we may not even realize the hurt and the pain we cause God when we are blatantly disrespectful, not *just* to God, but also to our parents, our neighbors, even to ourselves. I believe it hurts the heart of God because we are an extension of Him. Plus, it hurts Him to see us hurting and destroying ourselves. He has given us wisdom, wise counselors, examples, forgiveness, help, and understanding. He has lifted us time and time again out of the pits; out of the holes; out of the struggles; out of the jails and prisons; and out of the over-whelming messes we've made of our lives. Like our children, we've fought against God's influence, the love of God, etc., wanting after the lusts of our eyes, the lusts of our flesh, and the pride of life.

I am striving to love my children as God loves me, in spite of it *all*. I believe, just like us, even when their intentions are good and they're not intentionally trying to be rebellious and disrespectful, they can still utterly miss *it*, especially when they don't have the wisdom and the Spirit of God leading and guiding their lives.

I understand too, sometimes things just don't make sense. People may feel as if God is too hard to figure out and understand. Well, so are we. The way we see things doesn't always make sense to our children just like God's ways are not our ways (*see* Isaiah 55:9). There are times when God doesn't answer or doesn't give us the answer we desire; times when God doesn't come when we think He should come; times when we can't recognize Him; times when God requires of us things we don't want to give or do; and times when God allows us to be hurt and to endure extremely painful situations.

We all want our children to see our efforts as desires to shield them, protect them, lead them, and help them; and our love for them as motivation to push them to succeed, to live blessed lives, to experience good, prosperous, peaceful, happy, healthy, and fulfilling relationships.

As parents, sometimes we miss it. Sometimes we don't make the best decisions or the right decisions either. Sometimes we need our children to forgive and cover us. I believe it is still to the children's benefit to respect their parents, even when they miss it. When Noah got drunk and was laying in his tent naked, one of his sons mocked him, but two of his sons covered him. They even walked in Noah's tent backwards, refusing to look upon his nakedness.

They reaped the benefits of honoring their father, while the other son was cursed (*see* Genesis 9:20-27).

It is so beautiful to see children honor and respect their parents with sincerity, innocence, and humility. I've seen how children look beyond the shame of a parent's drug addiction; the struggle of a debilitating disease; the pain and shame of being poor or home-less; and other heart wrenching issues to cover their parent's nakedness. God's Word teaches that child-ren who honor their mother and father can even lengthen their lives.

> 'Honor your father and your mother, as the Lord your God has commanded you, that your days may be long, and that it may be well with you in the land which the Lord your God is giving you.[']
>
> -Deuteronomy 5:16

I know it is sometimes challenging for children as they are learning to establish their own boundaries and learning to make their own decisions. Growing and maturing into adulthood demands a certain level of independence and even separation. But when decisions are challenged or there are differences of opinion, children should always deal with their parents with the utmost respect; especially those still living in their parents' home.

As parents, we must realize and acknowledge that we can provoke our children, although we should not (*see* Ephesians 6:4). I believe we do share some of the responsibility for their decisions because of things we did and didn't do and some of the things we failed to teach, and instill in them; even if it was due to our own ignorance or bad decisions. I believe we still share a big part of how they are shaped and developed. Some say when they are adults, they are responsible for their own choices, and bear the consequences of their own actions. While that's true, I don't believe it means we are completely innocent of how we impact and have impacted them during the most influential and formative periods of their lives. I believe God can still cause things to work together for good as we grow and learn, and as our hearts are matured, healed, and repentant.

Jacob showed favoritism to Joseph over his eleven other sons. It affected their attitudes toward Joseph and their brotherly relationships with him. Jacob, in his heart, may have just been showing love to Joseph and covering him because of the love he felt for Rachel, Joseph's mother, but still it provoked the other sons to mistreat Joseph. He even gave him a special coat (*see* Genesis 37:3-4). In the end, God worked it for good, but look at how it caused Joseph's brothers to be hard-hearted and divided from him for so many years. It is amazing to see how God can turn situations around and mature us even through suffering and the mistakes we make. God can even make things better than they were and heal all hurt from the past; restoring relationships we thought were beyond repair. I love how God even allowed Jacob to know Joseph was not dead, and see him again, as well as Joseph's children (beyond what he could have imagined). Joseph was thrown into the pit to die, then sold into slavery (*see* Genesis 37:23-28). He had every right to hate his brothers and to hold a grudge for all that he had suffered, but through it all, God had him covered. Through it all, Joseph maintained the right heart toward God, and God never left him. In the fullness of time, God rewarded Joseph for enduring hardness as a good soldier (*see* 2 Timothy 2:3-5) and allowed him to be restored to his family. We don't know all the reasons why God allowed those things to happen. We don't know why God allows all that He allows in our lives. But, like Joseph, our goal should be to trust God, keep a good attitude, and keep our hearts pure from malice, unforgiveness, bitterness, resentment, and giving up on God.

As children, we can remove ourselves from the covering of our parents and suffer greatly, like the prodigal son. He just wanted to live his life! He obviously did not give enough thought to the consequences of his choices, and ended up losing everything, even desiring to eat what the pigs were eating to stay alive (*see* Luke 15:13-16). Many children have run off in rebellion and struggled greatly. Absalom rejected the guidance and discipline of God and of his father, and ultimately lost his life (*see* 2 Samuel 15:10-12 and 2 Samuel 18:9-10). Eli failed to discipline his children and their choices affected generations (*see* 1 Samuel 3:13-14). As parents, we can fail to cover our children by not disciplining them as we should, by not correcting their wrong behavior and rebuking them when they need a strong rebuke; even by continuing to look past their bad attitudes and disposition. Either way, the consequences of our actions or refusal to act can be extensive.

We know every situation is not the same, so we can't treat every situation or every child the same. I believe our motives and our attitudes, as parents, makes the difference. Moses' mother took the chance to release him from her covering and entrusted him to God; even while he was just a baby and completely helpless (*see* Exodus 2:2-3). If he had stayed with her any longer than he had, she could have jeopardized his life completely. Her heart was innocent of any intentional neglect. She was completely at the mercy of God. Abraham had to remove his son, Ishmael, from his care (*see* Genesis 21:14). Abraham's heart also was innocent of any malicious or uncaring intentions. Ishmael was also innocent; they truly trusted in God.

In another story, two women both had babies three days apart, and one of the babies died. When the woman whose baby died tried to claim the other baby, the baby's real mother was willing to give the baby up rather than let the baby's life be lost (*see* 1 Kings 3:16-28). In these situations, the children were uncovered although their mothers greatly desired to cover and protect them. Sometimes, all we can do is cover our children in loving prayers and supplications to God.

My prayer for children everywhere is that they would embrace the will of God and cultivate their desire to obey God, believing God will reward them for their obedience, honor, and respect. I pray that parents will continue to love and cover their children, even when they are wayward and rebellious; even when circumstances beyond their control have caused their children to be apart from them. Our prayers and love can make the difference in them coming home, surrendering their lives to Christ, being kept safe, and making detrimental decisions. I pray God will restore and turn relationships around for good where there has been painful divides and struggles. I pray, *what the enemy meant for evil, God will turn around for good* (*see* Genesis 50:20). I pray that we remain submitted, continuously; that we trust when we don't understand; that we continuously love, despite what we feel; that we keep our hearts open and surrendered to God; and that we all continue to grow through every experience and overcome, no matter the trial.

Uncovered

(longing to be covered)

Uncovered, no one to watch over and care for your needs
to protect you from dangers seen and unseen
No one to lead you through to greater things

Uncovered, no one praying over your soul
No one to guide you through the unknown
No one there for you when you feel alone

Uncovered, vulnerable to the evil things
To the enemy's wicked and perverted schemes
To the attacks on your plans, your goals, and your dreams

Uncovered, prey for those who would consume the weak
For those who know you can't discern the thief
for those who lie, kill and cheat

Uncovered, can't hardly wait for the morning light
To be sheltered from the dark of night
From the deceptive wrongs that look and feel right

Uncovered, the years of needing and longing
The struggle of waiting, searching, and wanting
Fearing what could come, the haunting and taunting

Uncovered, exposed to the winds and rain
Storms and heartaches, the danger, and pain
Worrying that things will never change

Uncovered, wanting to hide, where can you go
Who really cares, who even knows
Is there really a place for your seed to grow

Uncovered, your hearts willing, ready, and ripe
hungry and thirsty, you surrender your life
you just want a love that's willing to try
A love that says you're worth the fight
A love like God's that will never die
A cover that feels just right

Chapter Three

A Spouse's Covering

I have another friend whose husband's love, I believe, healed her. She was sick with cancer. At one point she was not even expected to live. I remember how when this man started showing an interest in her, she could not even entertain the idea of dating because she was so sick. But he wasn't scared off by it and he didn't go away. He stayed with her at the hospital and tended to her like one of the nurses and during this time they were just dating. He not only healed her with his love, but he won her over with his love. Deuteronomy 28:2 says, "And all these blessings shall come upon you and overtake you, because you obey the voice of the Lord your God:" To me, that means literally chases us down! That *harlequin romance stuff* we feel like only happens in novels or in the movies. But I witnessed it for myself. They eventually married and now over ten years later they are still together. I'm convinced the love God gave him for her protected her, covered her, and ultimately healed her. I knew how sick she was. She even shared with me that at one point she felt like she wanted to die! At this point, I don't believe she even had faith for a husband.

As I talked about in the introduction, I have longed for the covering of a husband. I can just imagine someone chasing me and overtaking me with that kind of love; determined to make me their wife, even against all odds. I think like many others, I may have at times disqualified myself because I made so many bad decisions and mistakes in my quest for real love and because I can see and know my imperfections. I imagine every woman wants the kind of husband who will go the distance; the kind who wants the world to know how much he loves you; the kind who will give himself as Christ gave Himself for the church; and the kind you never have to question whether or not their love is real - *authentic and genuine love*, the kind that wipes away your insecurities; the kind that longs to take away your heartache, even sickness and pain; the kind that makes you want to be the best wife in the world; and the kind that allows you to be naked and not feel ashamed. Even though it may be hard at times to imagine, and even though that kind of love may be rare, I do believe it is real and that it still exists.

I don't think women who are covered really think enough about all they are covered and protected from. I heard one of my friends complain because her husband didn't want her out of the house when it got dark. In her defense, she's a grown woman, and she was taking care of herself before he came along. But to the woman, who has been afraid to come home to a dark house and afraid to have to leave the house at night because she realizes the dangers and how vulnerable she is alone, I imagine what she wouldn't give to have someone want to cover her that way.

Another one of my friends talked negatively about her husband's advances toward her. I understand, we can all get tired and sometimes we are not in the mood. I just want to admonish you, as *that* woman who would love the opportunity to get tired and not be in the mood (lol), be careful how you deal with your man in that moment. To be desired is a beautiful feeling, and an honor.

I believe a godly husband, not only covers his wife spiritually, but also from the longing and dangers of singleness (i.e., deception, manipulation, financial struggle and burden, single parenting, vulnerability, imbalance, compromise, spiritual challenges, insecurity, and a load of other emotional and physical challenges that can result due to the longing from being alone and uncovered; some realized, some unrealized). He also covers her physically with his strength.

I've often tried to do things around the house that were simply too hard or too heavy. A woman's strength simply cannot compare to a man's.

They can also cover us from having to partner with another woman or vice versa. I know some people think a female roommate could be good to just share the home and responsibilities, but trust me, no other balance can compare to a man and a woman.

When God said, "It is not good for man to be alone," I don't believe He was talking about just males, but mankind (*see* Genesis 2:18). Although I believe it is much more common for women to suffer from being uncovered than men, there are men who suffer some of the same challenges women face. However, the degree to which men suffer is not the same for (most) men. For example, most men are able to support themselves financially. Though it may not be a major issue for them, two are still better than one. Comfort and security are still better with a partner. And women can also help keep men from mistakes often made from their vulnerable feelings of longing and loneliness, as well.

While in many relationships, women are the ones who cover their families in prayer, both men and women can benefit greatly when they cover each other in prayer. Equally yoked partners help keep a balance spiritually; and especially sexually. The Bible says that all other sin is outside the body, but when we sin sexually, it is against the body (*see* 1 Corinthians 6:18). I don't understand all the reasons why, but when a woman falls sexually the world is much more judgmental against her than when a man does the same. Maybe it's psychological, but it's real, even if we can't understand it or explain it. Maybe it's just the mindset of mankind. Whatever the reason I think most will agree this point is true. Nevertheless, there are still spiritual repercussions.

I've heard it said before, and I agree, that more than anything women want to feel secure in every way: emotionally, physically, financially, spiritually, socially, etc. A woman feels love when she feels secure. We know ultimately, God is the one who keeps us safe, but God uses people in the earth. We can say thank you to God, but we also need to say thank you to those who provide and who make us feel safe, secure, loved, desired, cherished, special, covered, etc. And thank you to those who don't mind buying the gifts, giving the affirmations, the compliments, the effort, the attention, and going the extra mile, listening to the cry of our hearts, and making the investment for love and security.

When the washing machine breaks; when the car breaks down; when the yard needs to be cared for;

when the walls need to be painted; when the sink gets backed up; when the roof is leaking; when the bills are overwhelming us; when we need someone to hold; when our need for intimacy is unfulfilled . . . we don't want to fall into the wrong hands. We don't want to be taken advantage of. Some of us have been fortunate enough to have our fathers, brothers, and even genuine friends to help us, and thank God for them. Women in the Bible were usually covered by their father, until marriage, then their husbands assumed all responsibility. I believe that's the way it should be, but no woman wants to be forty years old still trying to be taken care of by her daddy! Not even thirty years old. Anyone who does is more likely dealing with some other issues. While women feel love when we feel secure, men feel love when they are affirmed and respected. Even when a man is doing wrong, if he is covered instead of exposed or rejected, he is more likely to trust and appreciate a woman for how she handles those situations. We must all realize there are also opportunities for women to cover and protect men (with our words, when we serve them, in prayer, when they are hit with life's challenges, and with our support).

While we all want and need to be covered, we still don't want to be covered with just *any* kind of covering. I often think about Leah, and the raw deal

32

she was handed (*see* Genesis 29). I wonder why her dad gave her to a man who clearly wanted someone else, and even more-so, her sister. Was she better off having some love than none at all? Was she that ugly?! Was there a purpose in it all beyond what our natural minds can perceive? Was she only good for making babies? Was her father concerned she wouldn't get married, or was he trying to get her under someone else's covering? Was God intervening? Whatever the reasons, I think if she had been as loved and covered as Rachel, she would have felt the happiness and fulfillment she longed for. At the same time, when I think about Rachel and see that even though she had the love and desire of her husband, he couldn't be all to her he wanted to be. He longed to give her a child and see her heart's desire fulfilled, but they realized, only God could fulfill their longing (*see* Genesis 30:2).

It's crazy, but I think it shows us our ultimate covering and fulfillment is still in God. I realize even when we have love and are covered by a spouse's covering, we still need our union to be under the covering and the blessings of God. Even in marriage, life happens, and we have experiences that are painful, bitter, hard, and devastating. Spouses must cover each other and be submitted to God's covering: His will, His authority, His wisdom and understanding, and His love.

There is so much more to be said about men and women, husbands and wives, covering each other. My hope is that touching on it will make us all more mindful and appreciative of a spouse's covering.

My prayer for those who are married, is that your marriages thrive and be fulfilling. May you keep your marriages covered in prayer and remain submitted to God. I pray for those who are married, but like Leah, still feel like you're alone. Let your marriages be strengthened by God, who will fix the broken places, make the crooked places straight, and use what the enemy meant for evil for God's good purposes. May peace reign where there has been conflict and restoration take the place of what has been torn down. For those desiring marriage, I pray God will prepare you, equip you, and satisfy your longing with the right partner. I pray God will remove all hinderances, all distractions, all doubts, and all insecurities. I pray for those who have experienced devastating relationships that have made you feel like you never want to try again. God is able to heal you and take what the enemy meant for evil and turn it around for good. I pray that what has been held up, will be held up no longer. I pray God blesses your obedience, as you submit to His will for marriage. May God keep you and deliver from all fornication, infidelity, perversion, masturbation, homosexuality, and sexual idolatry. I pray for genuine love and unity in marriage. Thank God for the entity of marriage and the spouse's covering when two become one.

For the man who is trying desperately to cover the woman who has had the covering snatched from her and the wrong covering too many times, I pray that you will not give up on her. I pray that you will realize how much she needs your healing, your covering, your all, and that you will not give up on striving to be that man!

For the woman who is frustrated with the men who have failed and neglected to fully commit and do the work needed to make you feel secure, loved, hopeful, cherished, and more, I pray you will not give up on your men, and that you will continue to cover them with love, prayer, encouragement, etc.

I believe with all my heart that as you sow, you will reap; in the due season, when it's time for the harvest; when it's time for her to now care for you or when the tables have turned and now it's him who needs to be covered.

Cover Us

Since I'm sharing there's one more thing I'd like to ask before I go

*This is for those who are looking at the ladies
and considering taking one home*

*Would you cover us instead of preying on our weaknesses,
please don't treat us like whores*

*Yes, we long for your touch and embrace,
but to be covered is what we need more*

*Would you cover us with your gentleness,
we've got so many wounds still tender*

*Would you cover us; our minds hold so many hurtful things
we really don't want to remember*

*Would you consider covering us with real love,
not just another rendezvous*

*Would you consider putting our needs before yours,
and dealing with us in Truth*

*Remember Ruth; she gleaned in Boaz's field,
unashamed, she humbly submitted*

*He protected her and provided for her
then made sure that she was well respected*

*In the evening she went in and laid at his feet,
she was vulnerable and in a way she proposed*

*He covered her, intending her good,
her vulnerability was never exposed*

*Instead he set things in order;
it spoke volumes to the man that he was*

His plans were to cover her and be fully committed;
he determined to give her true love

She took a chance on him and was rewarded;
what if we take a chance on you

How will you treat us and how will you leave us;
feeling cherished or feeling misused

Will you cover us in good times and bad;
or for you is it just another game

Will you cover us in sickness and health;
or will you only add more to our pain

Will you cover us for richer or poorer;
or just look out for your own self

Will you cover us for better or worse;
or leave us pursuing somebody else

Yes, to cover us is a great price to pay;
I'd like to think of it as a good investment

What you sow in our lives, you'll reap;
if your seed is good, then a good inheritance

And yes we've heard a million times,
how men love sex, so here's a tip

We love it just as much as you;
you'd be surprised what we could give

We really do want to please you;
we really want to be on your team

We want to be your partners, lovers and friends;
all we need is for you to agree

We're vulnerable just like a flower;
easily bruised if you're not gentle

We'll give you beauty and a sweet aroma
if you take care of us; it's just that simple

So one more time, I'm asking you please,
to think on what I'm sharing today

We need love, protection, leadership and guidance
and we need to be covered God's way

What you plant in us will grow, and we're eager to produce;
we're not stupid, worthless or fools

We're a product of the things sown in our hearts,
so give us what you want us to produce

We need security and to be desired

We need love, we need respect

We need affection and honesty

We need patience and fulfillment

If you can hear us and if you care
your loving actions will let us know

God's Word can't lie; and it promises you
you will reap what you sow

Chapter Four
Covering Ourselves

More than ever, in this season, I realize it's necessary to cover ourselves properly. Stepping out of our comfort zones; from the place we've been for so long, leaves us feeling vulnerable and definitely without covering. We may want to run back to the safety we've known, but I believe there are times when it is necessary to make those life adjustments that may cause us to leave the comforts we've known for various reasons.

We must be assured that God knows where we are, even if we don't. We must believe God is with us despite our fears, insecurities, uncertainties, and struggles. Even despite those who question, doubt, or disagree with our decisions. Like children growing up and leaving home to develop in some other ways, it may be time for a new season. It can be scary; especially for those who God is calling out but has not given a clear direction of what to do next.

In this season, there may be times when we will not have anyone to cover us the way we have been accustomed to. In this season, we may have to put into practice what we have been taught and admonished to do concerning covering ourselves. It is very vital for us to practice covering ourselves: our eyes, our ears, our hearts, our bodies, and our possessions. We must practice as we have been trained, to respect ourselves, cover ourselves, and love ourselves. We must adhere to the teachings and the wisdom we've received from God, our parents, and those who have invested in our development and our futures. In this season, we can clearly see the difference love, honor, discipline, obedience, humility, and submission can make. For some, unfortunately, there may be an inability to comprehend the difference between being covered and being controlled. And some unfortunately, will continue to rebel against the teachings and the disciplines of God, others will adhere.

I can remember as a teenager trying to follow the fashion of the times. The clothes I wanted to wear; my dad did not approve of. In my defense, it was the style and what many others were wearing. In his defense, he knew how it would cause me to be preyed upon by those who would see only flesh and desire to devour me. For some dads, it's easy to shut it down, and leave no room for discussion. For some dads, who have such great relationships with their kids and a wonderful influence over their children, it only takes a loving conversation. For some though, who don't have the discipline or the loving relationship and lack the ability to properly cover, their kids are subject to exposure. Some kids will learn the hard way what it is to cover themselves; hopefully and prayerfully before they are consumed.

Sad to say, this is not just a lesson for children. There are many ladies, even older women, who never learned to properly cover themselves. As a result, many have been warped and deceived in their minds, covered by an improper influence and wrong teachings, and who are still uncovered.

Even when we realize how important it is for us to properly cover ourselves, it is still challenging. Many of us crave to be accepted, to fit in, to please, to be complete, and to be desired. Such unfulfilled longing can unknowingly cause us to *not* cover ourselves as we should. When we fail to have a proper self-image, it greatly impacts our ability to properly cover ourselves. It can cause us to open ourselves up to all kinds of influence and manipulation. Unfortunately, even when we seek guidance and wisdom, we can still be misled and illy influenced. So many have been greatly exposed to perversion and extreme wickedness due to longing and hoping, that someone will cover us, and failing to cover ourselves.

So many profess to be wise who are not wise. So many think their ways are right, but they are deceived. Sometimes it is very hard to know who to follow, and who to trust. Even parents can be on the wrong track and cause their children to be trained improperly. That's why even children sometimes must learn to cover themselves, and even to cover their siblings, friends, parents, and others. I would like to encourage us to think deeply about a few critical self-reflection questions:

- *What* does it mean to cover yourself?
- *How* can you cover yourself?
- *When* is it okay to uncover yourself?
- *Who* should you look to cover you?

There have been times I really felt I needed others to cover me, and there are times when I still do. But for the most part, I understand there are times when others won't be there to cover and protect us. We must prepare ourselves to properly respond when we are lied to, deceived, unappreciated, under-valued, rejected, vulnerable, and if we're not careful, preyed upon. It is vital for us to learn to cover ourselves and not underestimate the extremes of being exposed.

When I started being able to date, I was approached not by boys my age, but by grown men, married men, players, manipulators, perverts, ... *you name it!* I didn't have a clue! I had been sheltered and covered, however not equipped to deal with the real world! I didn't know God! I didn't know the Scrip-

44

tures! I didn't have the proper covering of a father or any older men! *Need I say more?!* I tried to cover myself, but honestly, because I had a low self-image, time and time again, I believed the lies. Time and time again, I uncovered myself to what I thought was love. I know I'm not alone.

Even in my latter years, it is hard to detect the counterfeit, the thief, the liar, the game, the deceiver, etc. It's still hard to maneuver through the longing for the covering of real love. I've continued to make mistakes and to suffer the consequences. The result of which is *more* disappointment and failure. It's hard knowing when to take a chance on love, and when not to. Some people take a chance and succeed, while others fail and continue to recoil. I believe the success is worth the risk, but we must be careful how we engage. Before we unveil ourselves and damage ourselves any further, or damage others, I pray we really take a good look at the *what*, the *how*, the *when*, the *who*, and really rely on the wisdom and guidance of God. Some additional questions to benefit from:

- How do you feel about covering yourself?
- Do you look for others to cover and protect you?
- Do you think the potential of success is worth the risk?
- How do you think you can engage safely?

There is a lot to think about. There is a lot at stake. If you've ever had a broken heart, you never want to go through that again! If you're like me and long to find real love, a covering that will endure, I admonish you to realize how serious the effects of being covered and uncovered can be. Finding anything other than real love can even be crippling. Because of the yearning in my heart, I long to see others find loving relationships, also. I have even thought about being a matchmaker, but I realize there is more to it than finding a person.

My prayer for us in covering ourselves is that we will do so with respect; not in shame and fear. Get rid of those negative coverings and refuse to wear them anymore! I pray even though we are endeavoring to cover and protect ourselves, those who are true potentials, will still be able to see our potential, our beauty, our assets, our hearts, our gifts, and our attributes. I pray when the time is right, we will be able to let our guards down and receive new covering as new wineskin; without bracing ourselves with fear of the potential impact of hurt and disappointment. I pray for those who have been uncovered to be covered, and for those who have lost hope of ever being covered, to believe again, and receive!

Chapter Five

Unseen & Unexpected Covering

Have you ever had someone just go to bat for you? Have you ever gone to bat for someone else; it could have been someone you didn't even know or who didn't know you? Have you ever just had *that* feeling others were praying for you? Have you ever just felt the need to pray for someone else? God can make a way - even use angels and strangers.

I believe we have all experienced times when someone stepped in to protect us, defend us, or speak up for us. It's a feeling that's hard to respond to; especially when we know how much of a sacrifice was made to do so. You can't help but wonder, are they really angels in disguise? Were they sent by God? Why were they so compelled to help or step in? Then, how should I express sincere gratitude? And vice versa when God is using us.

We all need those unexpected coverings, and at times to be those coverings; financially, physically, socially, and especially spiritually. Sometimes those miraculous coverings can even come from the most unexpected people. Yes, we should be grateful, but I believe there's more for us to see and realize. Specifically, nothing is too hard for God. No one is without hope or the ability to be helped, loved, restored, healed, protected, forgiven, cared for, etc., We never know when and how God will show up.

The Bible tells us to be careful when we entertain strangers, for we may be unknowingly entertaining angels (*see* Hebrews 13:2). That's so true. God can use anyone and turn any situation around. It is amazing what God can do, has done, and will do!

The Hebrew boys were in the fiery furnace (*see* Daniel 3), but the Bible tells us there was another person in the furnace with them and the form of the fourth was like the Son of God. They were delivered from the fire without harm; not even smelling of smoke.

I've seen beautiful relationships develop in situations where initially the woman wasn't attracted to the man and had no interest in him. But because she was careful how she responded to him and treated him, she found there was more to that man than she could ever have imagined. When a person loves and cares for you, they are hard to overlook. When we feel covered and safe, it's hard to replace or ignore those feelings. We all want our hearts to be protected.

As far as I know, I'm not adopted naturally. But, I can imagine a child who doesn't have a family, receiving a family, inclusive of unexpected hope, joy, protection, provision, etc. I believe that's what God has done for us, and continues to do through miracles, angels, strangers, and even those encounters we can't explain (even in His adoption of us).

I do believe in angels. *Can I say I've ever seen one? Can I say I haven't?* I've heard others share their testimonies of being covered or protected by some unseen force. It's inspiring to think there are angels watching over us; even as we sleep. And even when we don't realize there is an imminent threat or danger. It's comforting and reassuring to know God has not only people assigned to us, but also angelic beings. I remember times when I felt like I didn't see God's face, but I saw His back after coming through some scary and potentially dangerous situations. With full assurance, I realized that God had been with me and that He brought me safely *through* (*see* Exodus 33:17-23).

I believe we are also covered through special relationships we develop or that come to us by whatever means. I've come to know some beautiful and wonderful people, who I know have the Spirit of God within them. People who have blessed me so much I didn't know how to receive it. I felt like it had to be God in them because I didn't in any way deserve it. I've had some who helped pray me out of depression; out of struggle and lack; out of trouble and messes I had gotten myself into; and out of hopelessness and discouragement. I've had friends and strangers who showed up as if on cue, to meet a need they didn't even realize they were meeting; and who were there to show unconditional love in a time of need. I hope to be used by God in those same ways for others more and more. It's times like those we can say, "It is truly better to give than to receive." It's refreshing when it's God working in us. When it's not God, or not done with the love and the heart of God, and we're trying to be there for someone in our own strength, it's frustrating. It can be draining, taxing, and anything but rewarding.

In Spite Of

Boaz didn't show up expecting to find Ruth
When he saw her, she captured his interest
Her character spoke volumes of who she was
He felt compelled to invest
He inquired about her, showed her favor
and intentionally cared for her needs
Who was she and what was so special about her
What was it that Boaz could see
Was it the God in her that stood out in his eyes
Or God in him working on him inside
I love this story and how it unfolds
especially how she lays at his feet
He could have taken advantage of her
But he cared for her dignity
He was gentle, attentive, and wise in the way
he responded to her vulnerability
The way she covered her mother-in-law
She had no idea she would reap
He wasn't just any other man
He had authority, character, and was kind
He respected and covered her though she was broken
Traits that are hard to find

He was her covering in every way
He was willing to do whatever it would take
She humbly submitted and things turned out great
She reaped from the humility she displayed
In spite of her past, in spite of her pain
Her character and virtue she humbly maintained
And when the time came for her to be covered
She was more than prepared for love to love her
In spite of his power, he wasn't full of pride
He was filled with goodness and love inside
He was willing and able to share all he had
When the time was right, he held nothing back
In spite of the expectation, they had
God too had a plan that would come to pass
He knew they were ready; He knew it was time
He brought them together with a plan so divine
Who could dispute that God was in the midst
Who else could perfect a plan like this
In spite of opposition and in spite of the odds
It wasn't too big or too hard for God
I hope this love story helps others embrace
the hope and the character that they displayed
When it's your time to give and your time to receive
May your harvest exceed what you hope to reap

Chapter Six
Not Alone

We have to know we are not alone in all our experiences. But I think we still often fail to realize we are covered in so many ways and that we need to be covered, as well as be a covering for others. Sometimes it can be too much and sometimes it can feel unwelcoming. Nevertheless, I think becoming more aware of our need to be covered; who we need to cover or let cover us; why, and the benefits thereof; invokes us to be more active and acceptive in the parts we play.

It is my prayer that little babies will be covered properly and gently. Our toddlers and teenagers will be better covered, and that they will not reject the covering they have been provided but realize more and more their need to be covered. Even as I think about how much they fail to realize how vulnerable they are, and how much they need to submit to those doing their best to cover them, I believe my level of expression doesn't even begin to describe all the reasons why they desperately need to stay close to the protection of God and to those assigned to watch over them.

I pray those outside the ark of God's protection and safety will come into the ark before it is too late. In the story of Noah's Ark, people were just doing what they wanted to do, while Noah and his family heeded to the voice of God (*see* Genesis 6:13-14). His wife didn't call him crazy. She listened to her husband and followed him. Their children also had the choice to follow their dad or leave; especially seeing how big the task was before them. Can you imagine your parents coming to you with a task that seems so outlandish or humanly impossible to do? What about your pastors and leaders trying to lead you in a way that seems utterly absurd? I don't think we could begin to submit or embrace God's plans or God's way of doing things without the Spirit of God within us or without allowing God to be our Father, our head, our covering, our help, etc.

Like rebellion and unbelief, there are many other things that could cause us to be out of the will, the alignment, and the protection of God. But I believe we realign through prayer, through submission and surrender, through hope, through trust, through wisdom and understanding, through the protection and covering other people may provide, through angels and unseen and unexpected forces, and more.

What if my insights and admonishment could make a difference? What if husbands and men saw them-selves as the covering for their wives and the women in their lives? What if women knew their prayers for their husbands could make a difference? How would she pray for him? What if we yielded to, instead of fighting against, those who endeavor to cover us? What if our efforts to cover others could make a difference? And, what if we understood and took the responsibility to cover ourselves during seasons of change, separation, and development? I am persuaded that even a child praying can make a difference. Even a child being the covering for another child could make a difference. Even a child speaking up and speaking out could make a difference.

I pray that God will give us insight and understanding, even the more, to be covered and to cover others according to His wisdom and His love.

I pray we continue praying for each other. I believe our prayers are heard. I thank God for hearing every prayer and answering as only He can. He has called us all to pray for all on all occasions and to love one another. This means to cover.

May we all be covered in the blessings of God!

When I started writing this book, I had no idea I would go through some of the extremes I've gone through. I felt compelled to get out of a relationship I had been in for years and basically out of my comfort zone. Although, I wasn't completely covered, I realize I did have a form of covering. It has been challenging in every way being out of even a partial covering, but I had to make the changes for a number of reasons. At the same time, I stepped out of my spiritual covering; also feeling compelled to make adjustments in that area of my life. Those decisions brought about some major challenges and emotions for me and also for those connected to me. I've also had career changes and challenges. Making these major changes in my life in some ways feels like faith, in other ways it makes me question my soundness and ability to endure. Either way, I'm out here. I feel vulnerable, uncertain, and desperate; while at the same time determined, hopeful, and mature. I'm praying and depending on God more and more to keep me covered knowing that God alone understands all the whys and challenges we all face in times like these.

I pray I will cover myself as much as possible. And I pray God will give me the covering I need as I strive to stay in alignment with Him, whether it's restoring the old and making things right; or establishing new relationships and coverings according to my needs and His will, in understanding, holiness, wisdom, love, purpose, etc.

For those who feel it is time to get out of the place you've been for whatever reason, I pray God give you all you need to face the challenges, the uncertainties, the fears, the doubts, and more till you see victory, keeping your eyes on Jesus.

Chapter Seven
Before the Covering

I was thinking about some of the reasons why many are uncovered; figuratively speaking. I see many push people away, many relationships doomed to fail, many lose hope and don't want to try again, or allow anyone else too close to their wounds. I believe it's because many people have not intentionally and effectively treated their wounds, which has kept the wounds from healing properly, and has even left some very unattractive scars they don't want others to see. Before bandages are applied, wounds should be treated: cleaned, ointment applied, and based on the severity some-times even given a certain amount of time to heal before a cloth can safely cover the wound.

As I look at my own life, so many times I have longed for the covering and looked for the covering before healing and before having my wounds properly treated or cleansed. Even when I've been advised to allow time to let the wound heal, I've found that waiting is very challenging for one reason or another. I've tried to cover the wound too quickly because I didn't want anyone to see it; at times I was embarrassed by it. I've tried to rush and cover the wound because of the inconvenience of having to deal with it; or because it was hindering me from doing something I wanted to do. Whatever the reasons we don't want to go through the process, or that we want to cover our wounds before they are treated and had a chance to heal, it can be very instrumental in why we continue to keep enduring the same kind of hurt, the same kind of issues and struggles, and the same kind of problems which ultimately leave us unhealed.

Going through the process of healing can be long, depending on the seriousness or the depth of the wound. But realizing and understanding we are wounded, that we need to get proper care or treatment, and then allowing ourselves an appropriate amount of time to heal before we cover those areas is vital. I'm beginning to understand this more and more.

We wear masks. We wear makeup. We want quick fixes and overnight wonders. We want God to stop the wind, move the mountains, send radical change and deliverance, and we feel overwhelmed because the process is taking too long, or we're not being covered fast enough. I'm talking about me! And based on some of the relationships I've witnessed and experienced, I know I'm not alone.

How many can trust God and His timing for the things we need and desire, and with the process that it takes for God to do what He needs to do in us, to us, and for us? How do we trust Him to fulfill our needs and desires? Sarai and Abram tried to help God with the promise He gave them. We have to admit, it did look like it was going to be too late, or like it wasn't going to come to pass (*see* Genesis 16:1-5). I believe we can all relate to some of what they were feeling, even to the point of trying to accomplish their dreams in their own strength. I think we've all been guilty of trying to take matters into our own hands. Trying to understand and figure out God can drive us to places of desperation, and desperation can make us do some crazy things.

In this season, I'm endeavoring to trust God to cover me and to fulfill the longing in me. I don't want to make the same mistakes I've made in the past, and I don't want to keep trying to cover myself and be outside of the timing and will of God. It's not easy. I feel anxious every day. Then I start to feel the pain of my wounds not yet healed, and the memories of how I acquired those wounds. I'm continually striving to bring my mind back to the place of submission, surrender, and trust.

I hope and pray you are encouraged to trust God's process and timing as He is working things out in your life. I know what it feels like to be overwhelmed with discouragement, hopelessness, weariness, longing, desperation, weakness, and even the pain of the process, but don't quit! Don't give up! Believe that trouble don't last always! Believe that joy comes in the morning! Believe that God can and will come through! Believe God!

Sometimes it's hard for us to remember all the times God has come through before. All the times He has blanketed us with His love; when He has given His peace that surpasses all understanding; and the comfort only He could provide. God has been there for us, even when we didn't realize it was Him walking beside us, Him shielding us, and Him keeping us.

For those who may be feeling uncovered and the discomforts that are associated with it, I pray you will be encouraged to hope again in God; encouraged to trust again the faithfulness and the timing of God; and built up in the hope that God will help you and keep you while He's working things out in your life.

Before the woman with the issue of blood was healed, she first believed if she could just get to Jesus she would be healed (see Mark 5:25-34). The blind men cried out for Jesus to heal them; disregarding what anyone had to say about how loudly they cried out, or the attempts to keep them quiet, and they were healed (*see* Matthew 20:30). Joseph waited and endured for years before God showed up and showed out in His life (*see* Genesis 41:42). Some days we cry because in this flesh, and in our emotions, the pain is real, but we know that God can . . .

If you have to cry, have your cry! If you fall, get back up! When the enemy comes against you like a flood, know that God will raise up a standard against him (*see* Isaiah 59:19)! Endeavor to endure the hardness as good soldiers (*see* 2 Timothy 2:3)! When you've done all you can do to stand, stand therefore (*see* Ephesians 6:13)! I'm encouraging you as I encourage myself; allow God to heal, to cover, and to provide you with the proper covering.

When God blesses you, remember to thank Him and not forget Him (*see* Deuteronomy 8:10-11). Remember to share your testimony with others so they will be strengthened and encouraged. Remember this for the next time you're going through, or you're feeling alone and overwhelmed in the process of what God is working out in you, through you, and for you.

About the Author & Additional Works

Babette Bailey is a four-time published worldwide author. Each of her unique works share the totality of her heart in different ways. From poetry to expounding on Biblical principles, as they pertain to women and God's desire for the family, to guided motivational life enriching devotionals, you and your loved ones will be positively impacted by her work, which is available in the form of books, personalized poetry for all occasions, calendars, and household decor. If you need help telling *your* story, contact Babette for a ghostwriting consultation.

Please contact Babette Bailey directly for personalized poetry, calendars, household decor, and ghostwriting services:

writeforyourevent@gmail.com

Search your preferred online book retailer for additional works by Babette Bailey:

November 16, 2020

A Glimpse Into My Heart is a collection of poems sparked by many different people, events, hopes, dreams, issues, and a lot of other things that have touched & impacted Babette's heart in different ways.

Just like our lives, like a good song, or like a fresh new idea that could go on and on in our minds, these glimpses are meant to open the heart, gently lift the heart, and bring a spark to the heart that will go on and on.

Babette is glad to have this opportunity to touch your heart by sharing her heart with you. You will not only be able to relate to many of the poems in *A Glimpse Into My Heart*, but you will be inspired, encouraged, lifted up, smile, and even laugh.

Babette Bailey is the mother of three now adult children and grandmother of five. She is the 9th born of ten brothers and sisters.

After writing privately for many years, the time has now come to give a *A Glimpse Into My Heart* to the world.

May 9, 2021

So many times, we feel like we've heard it all before; we've got it all together; we know what we're doing; we're equipped and ready; or like everybody is wrong, except us.

We have even experienced times when we didn't want to hear another teaching, another preaching, another prophesy, or another video. We didn't want to read another book, another article, or another story. And we surely didn't want to talk about it anymore!

I want to encourage you to give it another try! Gather the women in your life, and let's embark on a continuous journey together to develop the *Ladies First* approach to life. This book is a compilation of life experiences, Scriptural truths, and authentic thoughts on matters of the heart.

December 21, 2021

Babette Bailey authentically shares her heart in her newest book of poetry, *Poetic Inspirations*. You are guaranteed to find encouragement, laughter, reasons to celebrate, and good ol' fashion unapologetic advice within these pages.

As you take a deep refreshing poetic breath, you will be inspired, renewed, and refreshed. There are tremendous amounts of love, strength, and positive wholesome messages in this book, heartfeltly prepared to be absorbed by women and men of all ages.

Next Chapter (excerpt)

You grew from just an infant, went from crawling to standing
From mumbling to chanting, from bouncing to standing
You learned to read and write, learned wrong from right
Learned to stand and fight, learned to embrace your plight
You've gone from chapter to chapter, from one situation to the next
From one song to another, you've always given your best
You've served and you've sacrificed, you put in your time and labor
You're about to begin the next chapter,
you're about to start your next adventure . . .

CPSIA information can be obtained
at www.ICGtesting.com
Printed in the USA
BVHW050327070223
658034BV00030B/515

9 781953 241429